T0288403

Helping Out in Summer

CONTENTS

NATIONAL GEOGRAPHIC School Publishing
Hampton-Brown

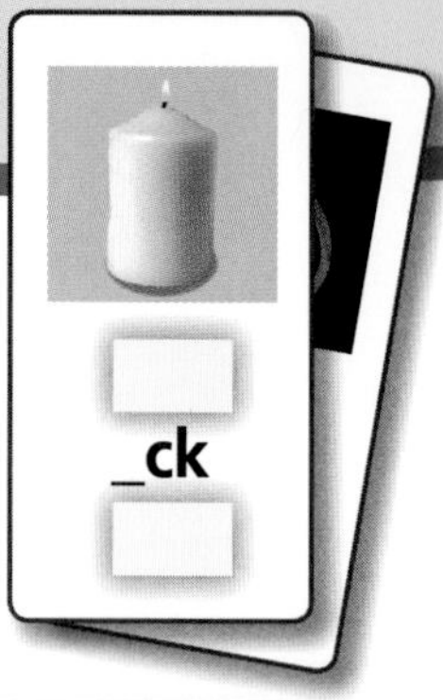

Consonants ck, ng

Look at each picture. Read the words.

Example:

pa**ck**

ja**ck**et

wi**ng**

sa**ck**

ri**ng**

ro**ck**

High Frequency Words

- each
- no
- said
- saw
- use
- was
- were
- who

Key Words

Look at the pictures. Read the sentences.

Here, Fang!

1. Rick and I **were** out when we **saw** Fang.
2. He **was** six blocks from Mom's.
3. We **each** **said**, "Fang!" But it was **no** **use**.
4. Then Rick said, "Fang! Let's get a snack!"
5. **Who** ran up and licked Rick's pocket?

How did the boys get Fang back?

Phonics Games

NGReach.com

A Bike Ride in Sun Falls

by Mary Bendix
illustrated by Don Tate

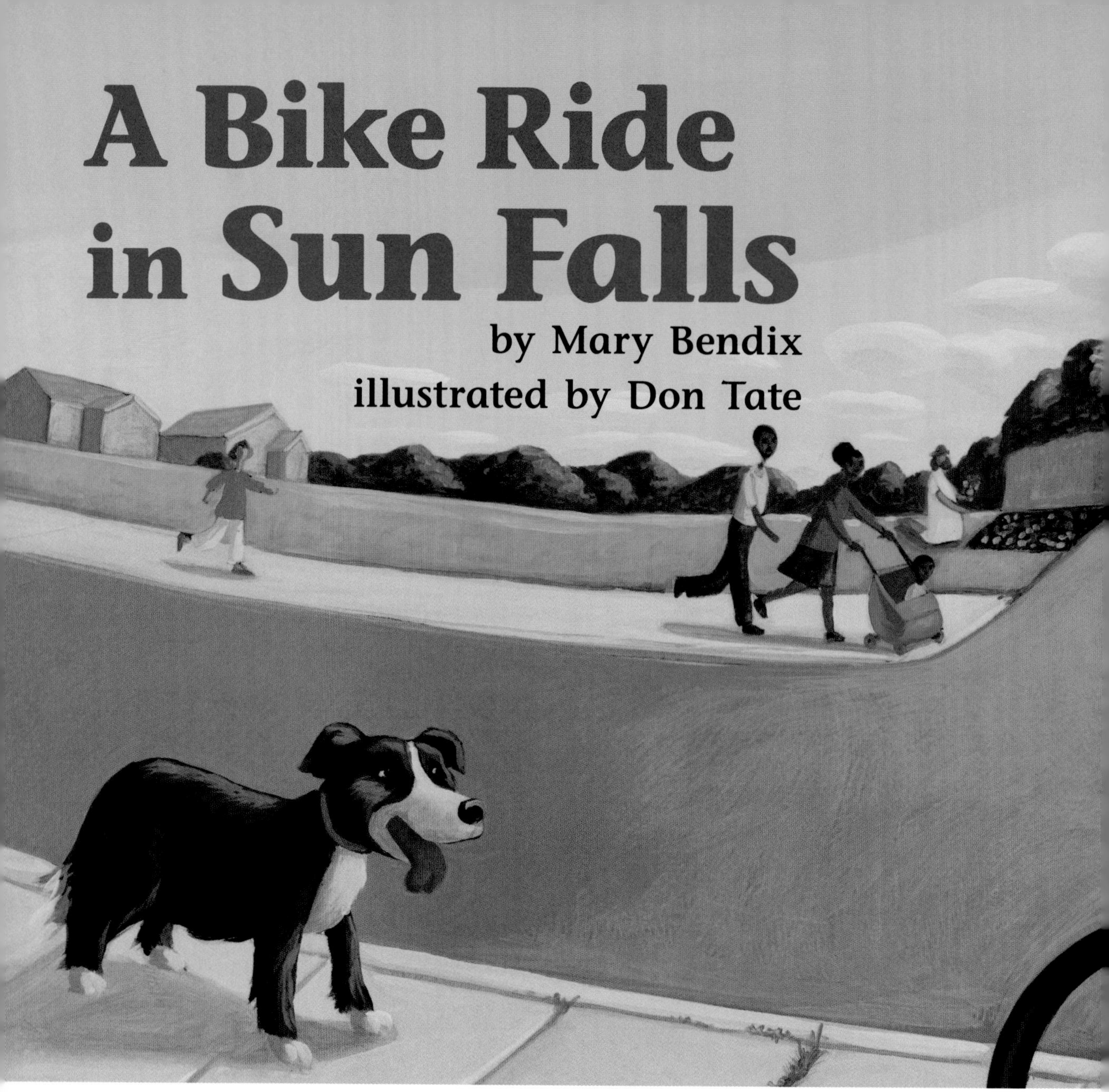

I went on a bike ride in Sun Falls.

There were lots of people to see.

I went down the hill on Red Wing Drive.
I said hello to Mr. Zack.

I saw him fix his fence.

I rode by the public garden. I got off my bike and said hello to Mrs. Vick.

Mrs. Vick let me pick a sack of carrots.
I had to tuck it in my pack.

I rode to the dock. I saw some men who had rods and a bucket of fish.

I sat on a rock. I fed each duck there.

Then I went up to the center of Sun Falls. I said hello to Mr. and Mrs. King. I had to help them hang up a basket. Mrs. King let me have a pack of gum.

I went to my pal Nick's. I rang the bell, but it was no use. No one was home.

On the long ride back home, who do you think I saw? Nick! He was out for a bike ride, too.

Consonants ck, ng

Read these words.

duck	kick	back	can	has
rang	swim	long	wings	flap

Find the words with double consonants **ck** or **ng**. Use letters to build them.

s i n g

Talk Together

Choose words from the box to tell your partner about each duck.

The duck can kick.

1.

2.

3.

Short Vowel Review

Look at the pictures. Read the words.

Example:

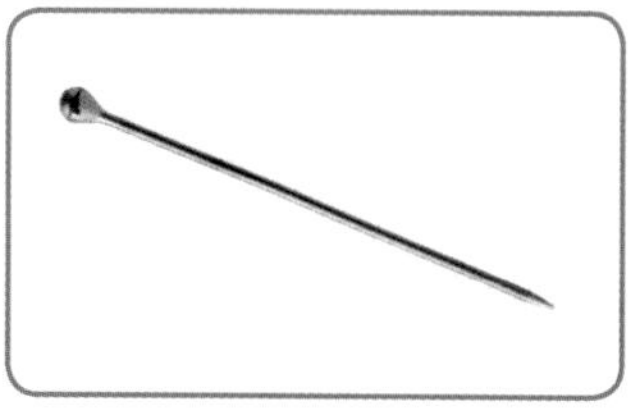

p**i**n

b**u**s

h**a**t

b**e**d

r**o**ck

w**i**ngs

High Frequency Words
each
no
said
saw
use
was
were
who

Key Words

Look at the picture. Read the sentences.

Rick's Backpack

1. **Each** summer we sell stuff on this block.
2. I **saw** a backpack at Rick's.
3. I **said**, "**Who** wants this?"
4. "**Were** you going to **use** it, Rick?"
5. "**No**," said Rick, "I **was** going to use yours!"

What can each kid use?

Phonics Games
NGReach.com

The 4th of July

by Maurice Patel
illustrated by Mircea Catusanu

We like to have a party on the 4th of July. We plan all winter long. It can be a big job, but it is a lot of fun.

Who helps? Lots of people help! Kids and their pals help. Moms and dads help, too.

We use a big box to make a puppet stage. Then we jazz it up with flags.

We use sock puppets to act out what was said on July 4, 1776. Tickets to see it will sell out fast!

There is a big picnic. Each person helps.

We have hot dogs and hot wings and corn on the cob.

We have a parade with a band.

We march with dogs and cats. Some kids ride bikes.

Then we have a lot of watermelon.

The day ends with a big bang!

July 4th can be the best day of the summer! ❖

Short Vowel Review

Read these words.

pocket	cap	sock	ring	pen
cup	napkin	pin	bucket	magnet

Find the words with short vowels.
Use letters to build them.

r i n g

Talk Together

Choose words from the box to tell your partner what Dan has.

Dan has a sock in his bucket.

Shop for a Picnic!

Kim and her Mom will have a picnic on their block. Help them get what they need. Put a marker on START. Take turns with a partner. Roll the dice and move your marker.

START

Who has the bags? No one? Go back 1.

Ask your partner to point to the big picnic basket. Get it and move 1 more.

DIP
You saw one pack of red napkins. Go back 2 to get it.
Get lots of hot dogs.
Ask your partner which dip he or she likes. Get it and move 1 more.
NUTS
There is no milk. Sing a sad song.
Pick a sack of nuts from the bin.
Get some eggs. Was one bad? Yes. Go back 2.
Go back 2 to get a bun for each hot dog.
Get ten cups to use for milk. Move 2 more.
$ 20.00
Get your bills out.

Acknowledgments
Grateful acknowledgment is given to the authors, artists, photographers, museums, publishers, and agents for permission to reprint copyrighted material. Every effort has been made to secure the appropriate permission. If any omissions have been made or if corrections are required, please contact the Publisher.

Photographic Credits
CVR Ariel Skelley/Blend Images/Getty Images. **2** (bcr) PhotoDisc/Getty Images. (bl) bluestocking/iStockphoto. (br) Richard McGuirk/iStockphoto. (cl) Andrew Howe/iStockphoto. (tl) Pei Lin Shang/iStockphoto. (trc) Roman Sigaev/Shutterstock. **3** Liz Garza Williams/Hampton-Brown/National Geographic School Publishing. **15** (bc) Martin Lukasiewicz/National Geographic Image Collection. (bl) Eric Isselée/Shutterstock. (br) Andy Gehrig/iStockphoto. (t) Liz Garza Williams/Hampton-Brown/National Geographic School Publishing. **16** (bl) Evelin Elmest/iStockphoto. (br) Ian Shaw/Alamy Images. (cl) John Foxx Images/Imagestate. (cr) Melissa King/Shutterstock. (tl) Milos Luzanin/iStockphoto. (tr) omers/Shutterstock. **17** Liz Garza Williams/Hampton-Brown/National Geographic School Publishing. **29** Liz Garza Williams/Hampton-Brown/National Geographic School Publishing.

Illustrator Credits
3, **17**, **29** Peter Grosshauser; **30-31** Mattia Cerato; **4-14** Don Tate; **18-28** Mircea Catusanu

National Geographic School Publishing
Hampton-Brown
www.NGSP.com

Printed in the USA.
RR Donnelley, Menasha, WI

ISBN:978-0-7362-8059-4

16 17 18 19
10 9 8 7 6 5 4